Defensive Investing Strategy of a Bond Man

MARK J. ANGIOLETTI

Txu 2-033-970

Table of Contents

Disclaimer 4

Dedication 5

Introduction 6

Chapter 1: 8

Know Your Self 8

Chapter 2: 12

Defensive Investing 12

Chapter 3: 15

The Foundation of Defensive Investment 15

Chapter 4: 21

Passive Defensive Investment 21

Chapter 5: 26

Aggressive Defensive Investment 26

Chapter 6: 29

Equity Investing for Aggressive Investors 29

Chapter 7: 36

Fixed Income for Aggressive Investors 36

Chapter 8: 43

Tradeable Derivatives 43

Chapter 9: 49

Closing Thoughts 49

Appendix 1: 52

Yield Calculations 52

Appendix 2: 55

Understanding Agency CMOs 55
Appendix 3: 57
Credit Ratings 57
Appendix 4: 60
Redefining Municipal Bonds 60
Appendix 5: 63
Insights to Quantifying Equity Valuation 63
About the Author 66

Disclaimer

The opinions expressed in this book are solely those of the author. No part of this book is to be construed as specific individual investment advice. The author of this book is not responsible or liable for any investment losses incurred by individuals attempting to follow strategies provided in this book. Investors should always consult with an experienced registered financial adviser before investing.

Dedication

This book is dedicated to investors looking to simplify investment strategy.

Introduction

My book *Fixed Income Insights of a Bond Man* provides readers a basic knowledge of fixed income securities. This book discusses the practical application of defensive investing.

Equities potentially provide inflation trouncing returns, fixed income securities provide predictable payments: a trade-off, investors often misinterpret.

Will Rogers, the depression era commentator, expressed a prudent investment philosophy with his comment: “I'm concerned about the return of my capital – not the return on my capital”. Investors that seek out-sized risk often fail to achieve their retirement goals – “Life isn't a race, it's a journey”.

Financial markets go through cycles – predicting the optimal asset allocation to maximize short term rate of return is exceedingly difficult as evidenced by professional hedge fund managers that frequently fail to deliver market beating performance. How can investors expect to achieve above average returns when professionals utilizing cutting edge strategies often fail to outperform the market?

No one can accurately predict the future – traditional asset management strategies direct investors to diversify by allocating a percentage of their capital to different asset classes[1] and assume financial markets will generate positive returns: Asset allocation strategies can limit exposure to one sector of the financial market, unfortunately most financial assets are positively correlated[2] and asset allocation strategies utilizing mutual funds[3] expose 100% of an investor's capital to risk, effectively increasing portfolio volatility.

Mutual fund diversification protects against security specific risk, it doesn't protect against market risk. Recent studies have shown global equity markets exhibit increasing levels of positive correlation[4] – prompting some investors to employ hedging techniques to reduce the impact of global equity market correlation on portfolio volatility[5]: Controlling equity market exposure is a more effective method of reducing portfolio risk.

Sincerely,

Mark J. Angioletti

---

1 Some readers will recall the asset allocation pie charts financial advisers use as a visual aid.

2 The price of positively correlated assets moves in the same direction.

3 Mutual funds often carry high embedded costs that can significantly reduce returns.

4 Global equity markets frequently move up and down in price together.

5 Some investors will recall portfolio insurance utilized during the late 1980's.

Chapter 1:

Know Your Self

Many investors learned the wisdom of not conforming to peer pressure yet bend to herd mentality when buying into the investment mantra of the moment[6] and experience catastrophic loss of capital.

Commodity traders have a saying "the trend is your friend" – when the trend breaks as it did in October '87, or during the dotcom / tech melt down of 1999 through 2001, investors learned no amount of commiserating[7] replaces lost capital: Experience is expensive.

Investors are unique individuals sharing similar emotional traits – the trait "safety in numbers", makes herd following seem like a logical strategy, but popular investment strategies often exhibit unacceptable levels of risk, how does an investor participate in the equity market while avoiding catastrophic losses.

Capital, what is referred to as money, can arouse strong emotions: only the loss of a loved one or a fatal medical diagnosis is more emotionally

---

6 *Extraordinary Popular Delusions and the Madness of Crowds*, Charles Mackay, pub. 1841, Richard Bentley, London

7 Misery loves company.

unsettling than a catastrophic[8] loss of capital. Risk control is paramount for investors to prevent emotions from influencing financial decisions.

Successful investing requires knowing one's risk tolerance – which can be determined by monetizing the loss $5,000, $10,000, $15,000, etc. – specific dollar amounts provide an investor the ability to calculate the percentage of capital a loss represents and an insight into the level of portfolio volatility they can comfortably tolerate[9]: Risk tolerance should define an investor's asset allocation strategy[10].

Forty-years of investment experience developed five basic rules to provide guidance in managing portfolio risk.

1st Rule

"Don't Lose Money" – this isn't an original idea[11]. Investors need specific reasons for investing that include investment expectations, time horizon, etc. The more accurately an investor defines their reason for investing, the less likely they are to

---

8 Capital that can't be easily replaced and will affect one's lifestyle.

9 The level of volatility that doesn't create sleep depriving stress, i.e. the sleep comfort level.

10 Investors can be passive or aggressive depending upon the time they can devote to investing.

11 Benjamin Graham the father of modern portfolio management was probably the first to express this.

panic over short term price fluctuation. Writing down specific investment reasons can be critical to controlling one's emotions.

2nd Rule

"Don't Forget the 1st Rule". Conforming with the 1st Rule is more difficult than it sounds. Financial market change can force investors to frequently review their portfolio, investment errors evaporate capital: Clearly define the reasons underlying an investment decision.

3rd Rule

Take your ego out of the decision process. Monetary loss has an emotional impact, introspection is a difficult part of the investment process: Knowing when to admit you made an investment error requires ego control.

4th Rule

Be Flexible. Portfolio decisions often require investors to quickly interpret new information, flexibility allows investors to adjust their portfolio to meet changing market scenarios while not changing strategy or risk parameters.

5th Rule

Investors are their own best line of defense. Financial industry regulators (SEC and FINRA) have implemented regulations requiring investment professionals act as fiduciaries rather than just transaction facilitators, but regulators can't prevent all investor abuse[12]. The financial services industry compensation structure can make it difficult for financial advisers to maintain professional standards: Always be an informed investor.

Adherence to rules requires a level of discipline investors may not be accustomed to, but it can provide protection from emotionally unpleasant experiences capital markets occasionally deliver.

Since "May Day"[13], the Financial Services Industry has utilized reduced commission rates to build client relationships. The low or no-commission approach has relevance for security transactions not based on financial advisers' professional input: Experienced financial advisers can provide investors with valuable decision-making information.

---

12 Regulators missed Bernard Madoff's Ponzi scam for the better part of 20-years, it wasn't until Madoff stepped forward admitting it was a scam that regulatory action was taken.

13 May 1st, 1975, the beginning of negotiated brokerage commissions.

Chapter 2:

Defensive Investing

Born out of the stock market crash of 1929 and formulated during the ensuing great depression[14] – defensive investing combined undervalued equities with fixed income assets to control portfolio risk. The primary axiom of defensive investing "margin of safety", was achieved by selecting undervalued securities; defined by low price to book value, low P/E ratio, or the ultimate bargain a net-net[15] (companies that can be purchased for the value of their current assets).

Investment analysis via quantitative parameters rather than hearsay, chart patterns, inside information, etc., was defensive investing's innovative change to portfolio management. Importantly, defensive investing was opposed to market timing – suggesting investors adjust their equity market exposure[16] by comparing the markets' earnings yield (the reciprocal of the P/E ratio) to investment grade bond yields when determining asset allocation[17].

---

14 *Security Analysis*; Benjamin Graham & David Dodd, pub. 1934, by McGraw Hill

15 Cash + Cash Equivalents + Collectible Receivables & Liquidation Value of Inventory – Total Liabilities = Net Net Value

16 Graham believed an investor should reduce market exposure as valuations rose not exit the market.

17 Asset allocation weighting being adjusted to take advantage the asset class with the higher projected rate

Defensive investing initially worked its way into the professional investment community via Benjamin Graham's course at Columbia University and with the 1949 publication of Graham's *The Intelligent Investor*[18] the discipline became accessible to non-professional investors. Additionally, Graham addressed equity market psychology by creating the persona "Mr. Market"[19] to illustrate the seemingly chaotic and irrational price swings equity markets often exhibit.

Defensive investing' quantitative method of adjusting equity exposure by comparing earning yields vs. bond yields to reduce equity exposure[20] during market bubbles was intended to control investors' emotions.

Equity market peaks are typically the product of misguided speculators[21] masquerading as investors. Speculation motivates investors to "swing for the fences" to garner market beating returns. Investors in control of their ego maintain their investment strategy.

---

of return.

18 *The Intelligent Investor*; Benjamin Graham, pub. 1949, by Harper & Row

19 Today, Mr. Market would be described as bi-polar.

20 Assuming an investors re-balances the asset allocation to reduce equity allocation as equity markets rise in value.

21 Seth Klarman coined the phrase investments throw off cash to their owners, everything else is speculating.

Over time defensive investing's quantitative analysis became ingrained throughout the Financial Services Industry and by the early 1970's Benjamin Graham[22] came to believe equity markets had become price efficient[23] – vastly different from the equity markets of the 1920's, '30s, '40s, and '50s.

Defensive investing like any investment strategy requires a commitment of time. Once an investor has determined their risk comfort level, they should realistically address the amount of time and effort they can devote to portfolio management: Passive defensive investors can implement the strategy with a minimal amount of time and effort, Aggressive[24] defensive investors need to expend considerable time and effort. The following chapters provide insights into application of both passive and aggressive defensive investing.

---

22 Graham is thought to be the father of modern portfolio theory.

23 Efficient Market Theory believes equity prices correctly reflect all known information regarding any security.

24 Graham referred to this as an enterprising investor willing to accept a businessman's risk.

Chapter 3:

The Foundation of Defensive Investment

Risk control is the heart of defensive investing – the key to controlling risk is a strong portfolio foundation. The traditional portfolio visual example is a broad pyramid base holding low risk assets (Treasury bills or cash) with a decreasing percentage allocation to riskier assets as you move up the pyramid. Controlling risk when utilizing a pyramid strategy requires actively reducing equity exposure during rising markets: Rising equity markets typically exhibit declining volatility that entices investors to increase risk exposure[25] as equity valuations are peaking, failing to protect investors at critical market junctures.

During the 1990s, the pie chart became the go to portfolio visual example, a strategy that purported to control risk via mutual funds diversification. Financial advisers don't generate fees from Treasury securities or cash so non-correlated assets were rarely utilized and pie chart allocations were composed entirely of positively correlated assets[26], exposing 100% of an investor's capital to market risk.

---

25 By allocating additional capital to equity exposure.

26 All the security prices moved together in the same direction.

Treasury securities are the only tradeable, interest bearing, non-correlated asset investors can hold in a portfolio. Treasury securities provide liquidity and rise in price during financial market panics (what is referred to as a flight to quality). Short-term Treasury securities (2-yrs. or less) are a risk-less alternative to cash.

Today's Treasury securities market[27] didn't exist when defensive investing was first developed – Defensive investing's creators[28] recommended holding investment grade[29] corporate debt or cash as an alternative to 100% equity exposure. The following information on fixed income securities is intended as an introduction to the subject, readers should refer to *Fixed Income Insights of a Bond Man* for a more detailed discussion.

U.S. Treasury Securities: Issued in 1-month to 30-year maturities (bills, notes, bonds) are backed by the Full Faith and Credit of the United States Treasury: have vanishingly low default risk. Treasury bills are discount securities with maturities of less than 1-year, Treasury notes are coupon bearing securities with maturities of 2-

---

27 Readers interested in the development of the Treasury securities market see Chapter 1 of *Fixed Income Insights of a Bond Man*

28 Benjamin Graham & David Dodd.

29 Before World War II the benchmark yield curve for U.S. fixed income markets was AT&T debt.

yrs. to 10-yrs., Treasury bonds are coupon bearing securities longer than 10-years. Currently, the Treasury holds weekly auctions of short-term cash management bills, notes, and bonds every month. With over $17 trillion of U.S. Treasury securities outstanding, the market for Treasury securities is the largest, deepest, most liquid securities market in the world[30]. Importantly, the Treasury Yield Curve, with maturities extending from less than 1-month to 30-years, is the benchmark yield curve from which other fixed income securities are priced at a yield spread to the corresponding maturity Treasury security. The pricing for spread[31] products (i.e. other fixed income securities) is quoted in basis points[32] to the corresponding maturity Treasury security. The basis point spread is a function of investment grade rating and prevailing market conditions. Lower credit rating securities are priced at larger basis point spreads to compensate for additional levels of risk.

Treasury Agency Securities: Issued by Ginnie Mae, Fannie Mae, Freddie Mac, and other Federal Agencies[33]. Ginnie Mae is part of HUD[34],

---

30 Treasury Securities are quoted in thirty-seconds, other fixed income securities are priced in decimals at a yield spread to the corresponding Treasury security.

31 The spread is the yield difference between a fixed income security and the corresponding maturity Treasury security.

32 1 basis point equals 0,01% hence 100 basis points equal 1%,

Fannie Mae and Freddie Mac are currently operated in conservatorship by the FHFA (Federal Housing Finance Agency)[35]. Agency securities are perceived as a secondary obligation of the U.S. Treasury, have very low credit default risk. Additionally, Ginnie Mae, Fannie Mae, and Freddie Mac mortgage backed (MBS) securities have monthly interest and principal payments backed by the Federal Housing Finance Agency.

U.S. Corporate Debt: Issued in various maturities with credit quality determined by credit ratings services such as Moody's or Standard & Poors[36]. Investment grade securities are rated Baa3/BBB– or above, securities rated below investment grade are High Yield (aka Junk Bonds)[37].

Municipal Debt: Issued by over 90,000 state and local borrowers in three basic formats; G.O. (General Obligation), Revenue, and Conduit bonds[38] are used to finance municipal

---

33 Additionally, the Federal Home Loan Bank and the Federal farm Credit Bureau.

34 HUD: Department of Housing and Urban Development.

35 For more information regarding Mortgage Backed Securities (MBS) collateralized by Agency insured mortgage pools see Appendix 2

36 Nationally Recognized Statistical Rating Organizations (NRSROs).

37 For more information on NRSROs' rating scales see Appendix 3

38 For more information regarding conduit issues see Appendix 4

government operations and essential services. Municipal securities generate interest that is exempt from Federal and in some cases State income taxes[39].

Foreign Sovereigns and Foreign Corporate Debt: Issued in developed and developing market economies. Most foreign debt securities are issued in foreign currencies causing them to have currency risk along with credit and interest rate risk. To eliminate currency risk for U.S. investors, some foreign issuers issue securities in U.S. $ denominations.

Aggressive defensive investors opt to allocate a portion of their capital to fixed income securities other than Treasuries are accepting a higher level of risk than owning non-correlated Treasury securities.

Investors attempting to provide liquidity at a target date typically purchase fixed income securities with maturities that match their target date in the mistaken belief they can divine the direction of interest rate change[40]: a misinterpretation of the Treasury yield curve.

---

39 Build America Bonds and other issues that qualify as Alternative Minimum Tax do not strictly pay tax exempt interest.

40 Even the Chairman of the Federal Reserve has difficulty diving the direction of interest rates.

The normal shaped Treasury yield curve (upward sloping to the right[41]) implies yields rise as time horizon increases due to the uncertainty of future inflation[42]: Shorter time horizons have lower affective yields – "rolling down the yield curve" is a term bond traders use to describe the effect of time on yield.

The normal Treasury yield curve (the most prevalent interest rate scenario) allows investors with a 1-month to 10-year time horizon invest capital beyond their time horizon and garner a higher current yield: As time passes, a security's maturity "rolls down" the yield curve allowing the higher coupon security to trade at a premium price to lower coupon current issue securities[43]. Investors often misinterpret the relationship of maturity and yield, preferring to increase portfolio income by reducing credit quality.

While investors can't accurately predict the direction of interest rates, they should utilize the yield curve to their advantage. Attempting to anticipate an interest rate rises over the last 35-years has misled many investors into low coupon short maturity securities often forfeiting the higher current income that would have accrued from longer maturities as they rolled down the

---

41 When plotting a normal yield curve time and yield increase as you move to the right side of the chart.

42 The name is derived from the fact that it displays the interest rate structure of "normal" economic conditions.

43 For a discussion of price vs. yield see Chapter 3 of *Fixed Income Insights of a Bond Man*.

yield curve.

Defensive investors requiring liquidity under all market scenarios should allocate a portion of their capital to short-term Treasury securities or cash. If income higher than short-term Treasury securities provide is required, a normal (positively sloped) Treasury yield curve will allow investors to utilize longer maturity Treasury securities to benefit from "rolling down the yield curve".

Chapter 4:

Passive Defensive Investment

Mutual funds, the Financial Services Industry's most recognized derivative product, became the go-to investment for Baby Boomers' IRA and 401K retirement savings during the 1980's.

Investment funds[44] were first developed in Europe during the 18th Century and closed end investment funds (CEFs) were issued in the U.S. in the late 19th Century. Open end mutual funds[45] weren't introduced into the U.S. until the 1920's, initially experiencing limited popularity. Before 1970, open end U.S. mutual funds held less than $50 billion, since the early '80s the combination of IRS tax code changes expanding the market for IRAs[46] and employer provided 401Ks swelled the amount invested in open end mutual funds to over $11 trillion – mutual fund management has persuaded investors investment success can be easily achieved by allocating capital to a combination funds.

The mutual fund industry's success in attracting

44 Three distinct type of investment funds exist: open end funds, UITs, and closed end funds (CEFs).

45 Open End Funds: mutual funds and its' newer cousin Exchange Traded Funds (ETFs) continually issue and redeem shares.

46 IRA regulations were changed in the early 80's to allow most individuals to open one.

investors capital was facilitated by seductive marketing tactics developed to promote multiple fund offerings with the message that professional management provides diversification and market beating performance at a vanishingly low cost. If mutual funds could deliver on their promotional hype, they would be a near perfect investment vehicle: reams of available data indicate reality doesn't match the fund industry's promotional hype.

The concept of professional management delivering market beating performance sounds enticing, but as Benjamin Graham pointed out it is exceedingly difficult to attain. Numerous studies have shown better than 85% of open-end mutual funds frequently underperform the market index they aim to outperform, and their claim of diversification is often illusory. Mutual funds ability to attract large amounts of investor capital forces fund managers to emulate herd mentality: most large mutual funds' top 10 holdings[47] are identical[48] and the embedded fee structure causes index lagging performance[49].

If index lagging performance is a result of embedded fees, why do investors assume mutual

---

47 Some will recall the pie charts that advocated buying multiple funds in a crude attempt to create diversification.

48 Large amounts of capital pouring into successful funds often can only be invested in the largest most liquid securities.

49 Embedded fees are delineated in the prospectus.

fund operational fees are insignificant: over time these fees significantly reduce investment return. Not surprisingly, some financial advisers exploit investors' lack of knowledge by promoting funds lacking upfront fees (no-load funds) as a strategy that will improve return[50].

If no-load funds allow 100% of an investors capital to be invested[51] why don't they always outperform load funds? Most investors are aware mutual funds have yearly management fees, what they don't know is mutual funds also have yearly marketing fees, directors fees, advisory fees, custodial fees, transaction fees, administration fees, auditing fees, legal fees, etc.; not all of which are listed as part of the fund expense ratio even though they are incurred[52] by fund shareholders[53].

When all fund fees and expenses are accounted for, the typical open-end mutual fund shareholder pays close to 2% per year in fees. A 2% average yearly fee structure allows the mutual fund industry to generate over $220 billion in annual revenues ($11 trillion x .02): which substantially reduces investors' rate of return.

---

50 A strategy that assumes no-load funds provide better management along with lower costs.

51 A sales load that ranged from 1% to as high as 8.5%.

52 Some fund companies temporarily absorb some fees to improve performance.

53 Most of these fees can only be seen by reading the legalese steeped prospectus.

In a global economic environment where many countries GDP growth is under 2% and financial market returns average less than 6% per year, the mutual fund industry's 2% fee structure implies investors are potentially forfeiting one third (2%/6%) of their potential yearly return. Why mutual fund investors agree to contribute 100% of the fund's capital, assume 100% of the investment risk, and agree to less than 100% of the return is difficult to understand.

Mutual funds' benchmark lagging performance along with their high embedded fee structure prompted some Financial Service Industry professionals to develop index funds: passively managed mutual funds holding only the securities that comprise the index[54] they attempt to mirror. Index mutual funds are a passive form of investing requiring no management input other than to adjust for changes made to the benchmark index, allowing their yearly expenses to potentially be lower. While the index fund concept was slow to catch on, today's investors are offered a wide variety index funds mirroring almost every index across the globe. Unfortunately, many of these index funds also have a high embedded cost structure.

An important change occurred in 1993 when State Street Global Advisors licensed the SPDRs[55]

---

54 The first one was Index Investment Trust on 12/31/75, later becoming the Vanguard 500 Index Fund.

55 SPDR pronounced Spyder is a registered trademark of Standard & Poors Financial Services LLC.

acronym (pronounced Spiders) from Standard & Poors Financial Services LLC to create the first exchange traded index trust (ETF[56]) based on the S&P 500 Equity Index. Initially listed on the Amex Exchange and currently trading under ARCA symbol SPY[57], State Street Global Advisors' SPDRs was the significant financial services industry product of the 1990's, providing investors access to an exchange traded index fund with continuous price discovery via intra-day trading coupled with a vanishingly low expense ratio[58]. Shortly after the SPDRs introduction, listed options and futures contracts were created that facilitated hedging and speculation on the S&P 500 Equity Index[59] price direction.

By utilizing SPDRs, defensive investors can easily implement a passive strategy that combines a diversified portfolio of equities and Treasury[60] securities – difficult to execute during the first nine decades of the 20th century. The only portfolio decisions passive defensive investors are required to make when utilizing SPDRs, is to re-balance equity capital allocation to adjust for changing equity market levels.

---

56 Exchange Traded Funds, ETFs can expand and contract their capitalization.

57 Later trading on the NYSE.

58 The SPDRs gross expense ratio is 0.1102% and net expense ratio is 0.0945%.

59 Since it is a broader based index than the Dow Jones 30 the S&P 500 Index is often referred to as market proxy.

60 Holding Treasury securities provides a non-correlated portfolio asset.

Since the inception of State Street Advisors' SPDRs, financial services firms have inundated the financial markets with a variety of ETFs[61], yet SPDRs remain the largest capitalization ETF due to a combination of important benefits: easy access to U.S. equity market diversification, the ability to adjust equity exposure during market hours, and hedge or short the S&P 500 Equity Index.

Today's passive defensive investors can easily implement the classic defensive portfolio allocation of 60% equities and 40% fixed income, while investors with a lower risk tolerance could implement a 40%/60% allocation, and investors with a higher risk tolerance a 75%/25% portfolio allocation.

61 U.S. based ETFs currently hold over $2.7 billion.

Chapter 5:

Aggressive Defensive Investment

Chapter 4 outlined the implementation of passive defensive investing: a strategy utilizing two asset classes, a diversified equity index fund (SPDRs, ARCA symbol SPY) and Treasury securities. The index fund provides equity market participation and Treasury securities provide liquidity while reducing portfolio volatility.

Risk control is a primary focus of all defensive investors[62] – defensive investing's first corollary "margin of safety" is the corner stone of controlling risk for investors venturing beyond the limitations of passive investing. The concept "margin of safety" is elegant in its simplicity, yet difficult for many investors to grasp.

No investment is without risk, but most investment strategies concentrate on an investment's potential gain, allowing investors to overlook the potential of loss. Focusing solely on potential investment gain often fails to address the potential of a negative outcome: the key reason for a "margin of safety".

Passive defensive investors circumvent individual security risk via a diversified index

62 Both passive and aggressive.

fund. Maintaining a "margin of safety" with a passive defensive strategy only requires re-balancing equity exposure as the equity market rises or falls. Passive defensive investing is a low-cost strategy that requires limited time and effort. Appealing as passive defensive investing is some investors desire a hands-on approach.

Unlike passive defensive investors' limited investment alternatives[63], aggressive defensive investors are faced with a wide array of potential investments; equities, fixed income securities, ETFs, REITs, royalty trusts, master limited partnerships, options, commodities, private real estate partnerships, timberland, oil wells, precious metals, gemstones, collectibles etc., some of which exhibit levels of risk or illiquidity suitable only for investors with specialized knowledge: Defensive investing's guidelines significantly reduce the number of viable investment choices.

Defensive investing advocates diversified equity market exposure, unfortunately aggressive defensive investors often end up holding a concentrated portfolio of non-diversified assets, for which defensive investing's "margin of safety" requires an expenditure of considerable time and effort on research. Fortunately, computerization of financial markets provides 21st Century investors easy access to price discovery[64] and information that reduce the

---

63 Listed Index Fund and Treasury securities.

expenditure of time.

Properly executing aggressive defensive investing requires investors expend time and effort selecting securities that meet a reasonable "margin of safety". Price discovery, a function of information and liquidity can conserve aggressive defensive investors time by narrowing the candidates to three broad categories: equities, fixed income securities, and tradeable derivatives; selection of which requires aggressive defensive investors have a passion for the security selection process.

---

64 The availability of both sides of a market (bid and offer): Liquid markets provide easy price discovery.

Chapter 6:

Equity Investing for Aggressive Investors

Equities are the financial media's most popular topic; consequently, more clichés exist regarding equity investment than other financial assets. Most investors are familiar with the color names; blue chips or red chip; the investment style descriptors growth stocks, stocks for widows and orphans, or the size descriptions small, medium, and large. Capital appreciation is the underlying reason for equity investment and defensive investing's "margin of safety" requires valuation parameters not clichés.

The use of quantitative parameters for security selection was defensive investing's groundbreaking innovation. Prior to the 1929 equity market crash, speculators invested on hearsay and inside information. The Securities Exchange Act of 1933 defined the use of inside information as illegal, radically changing equity market trading prior to the publication of Benjamin Graham's seminal investment text *Security Analysis*, in 1934.

Defensive investing's use of quantitative parameters encourages investors to analyze P/E ratios, price to book, EBITDA (earnings before interest, taxes, depreciation and amortization), dividend yield, etc. when searching for undervalued investments. Modern security markets continuous stream of information makes it difficult for an investor to legally gain an edge.

Equity markets gauge performance by price change, which is driven by revenue and earnings growth[65], the rate of which is often related to corporate size: corporations exhibit a life cycle over which earnings growth regresses to the mean[66].

Reversion to the mean[67] is a statistical measurement that can be applied to any group of subjects (in this case publicly traded corporations), with any statistical grouping you have what are referred to as outliers, subjects whose performance is either above or below the mean, eventually all surviving[68] subjects regress to the mean.

Successful businesses begin with an entrepreneurial vision and progress over time into a mature business. New businesses typically exhibiting higher growth rates than mature businesses. The application of "margin of safety" requires a realistic evaluation of a corporation's projected growth rate to determine fair equity pricing. Since corporate growth rate is often related to corporate size, it is important defensive

---

65 Since markets are forward looking current prices anticipate future rates of growth.

66 Typically, GDP growth rate.

67 The central tendency of a probability distribution, in this case the arithmetic average.

68 Failures occur in any group of subjects.

investors consider capitalization size[69] when attempting to project realistic growth rates.

Financial Services Industry's research generates earnings projections for actively traded equities. Based on earnings growth projections, research analysts determine if an equity is overpriced or underpriced. Unfortunately, analysts' projected growth rates can be very inaccurate. Defensive investors were advised to average 10-years of actual earnings (a complete economic cycle) to calculate what was referred to as "normalized" earnings.

The Federal Reserve's[70] actions over the last 40-years have muted the normal economic contraction and expansion cycle, forcing P/E ratios and earnings projections to tilt upward. Over time the concept of "normalized" earnings calculation was refined into the Cyclically Adjusted Price Earnings Ratio (CAPE), calculated by dividing the current S&P 500 Equity Index valuation by the 10-year average earnings of the S&P 500 Equity Index. CAPE is an inflation adjusted indication of the average corporate earnings multiple of the Standard & Poors 500 Index, not an individual equity, and provides a benchmark P/E ratio that can be utilized as an indicator of equity market valuation.

---

69 The number of shares outstanding times the current price per share.

70 Think of the unprecedented Fed Funds rate adjustments along with Quantitative Easing.

If every successful corporation's growth rate eventually slows, it is important investors consider a corporation's size (market capitalization[71]) before accepting earnings growth projections. Market capitalization is a parameter many investors deem unimportant when selecting investments. Most investors have heard the terms small cap., mid. cap., large cap., etc., but can't clearly define what they mean. The traditional definitions have generally been as follows;

Large Capitalization

$10 billion and over

Medium Capitalization

$1 to $10 billion

Small Capitalization

$250 million to $1 billion

Micro-cap

$250 million and under

---

71 Market Capitalization is calculated by multiplying the price per share by the number of shares outstanding.

With individual equity capitalization's heading toward $2 trillion, it is appropriate to redefine equity capitalization categories that provide insights into determining realistic earnings growth rate projections. Redefining categories has the potential of providing investors insights into realistic growth rates and potential merger or buyout candidates.

Ultra Large Cap

$1 trillion +

Very Large Cap

$250 to 1 trillion

Large Cap

$50 to $250 billion

Emerging Large Cap

$25 to $50 billion

Mid Cap

$10 to $25 billion

Emerging Mid Cap

$5 to $10 billion

Small Cap

$1 to $5 billion

Micro Cap

$100 million to $1 billion

Nano Cap

Under $100 million

P/E ratio, price to book, EBITDA, dividend yield, price to sales, debt to equity, etc. are important parameters investors should consider in equity selection, but only equity capitalization provides realistic insights into earnings growth.

Price appreciation isn't the only reason for owning equities: dividends comprise about half of the yearly return of the S&P 500 Equity Index. The S&P 500 Index is composed of companies in various stages of their life cycle and typically exhibit lower dividend payout ratios[72] during the growth stage of their life cycle than during the mature stage. Statistical studies on dividend payout has shown dividend growth rate is an indicator of free cash flow[73]: dividends can only be paid out of cash[74] hence dividend growth rate provides an important insight into earnings

---

72 The per share dividend divided by per share earnings.

73 An indication of a corporation's ability to operate without the need for external debt financing, i.e. leverage.

74 During low interest rate cycles some corporations increase operating leverage by borrowing to pay cash dividends.

growth.

Corporations exhibiting high levels of free cash flow without the use of excessive leverage can finance expansion from earnings. A corporation's board of directors decides what percentage of earnings are retained for investment or paid as dividends: Dividends are a tradeoff between reinvestment for future growth and current payout. Equities exhibiting high free cash flow and high dividend growth often trade at a premium P/E ratio to the S&P 500 Equity Index.

From inception, defensive investing embraced the ideology of bargain hunting, as markets became more efficient, bargains[75] became scarce, leading some investors to simply select equities trading at P/E ratios below the average equity market multiple. This type of bargain hunting typically steers investors into a value trap[76]: a mature corporation with an attractive dividend yield needing financial restructuring to restore earnings growth. Defensive investors should wait for a corporate restructuring announcement before committing capital to a potential value trap.

75 Recall Graham's net-nets

76 High dividend payout ratios can prohibit a corporation from investing in the future.

Chapter 7:

Fixed Income for Aggressive Investors

The financial media loves to denigrate fixed income securities. Over the last 40-years investors have been bombarded by media pundits proclaiming interest rates were rising and bond prices would be decimated[77]. With countless investment tomes advising only equities will outpace inflation, why would investors ever own fixed income securities?

Few investors recall the high inflation of the late '70s & early '80s, when large capitalization equities drifted lower in price and only emerging growth companies exhibited price appreciation[78]. Investors who held large cap. equities in the belief they would maintain value in the face of inflation were disappointed: only short-term Treasury securities exhibit price stability during periods of rising inflation.

My book *Fixed Income Insights of a Bond Man* discusses the U.S. Treasury yield curve[79] as the benchmark from which other segments of the

77 Where is it written interest rates must go up?

78 Investors may have heard about casino stocks or other story stocks.

79 Graphic representation of maturity vs. yield from less than 1-month to the 30-year maturity.

fixed income market are priced at a basis point spread to the corresponding maturity Treasury security – changes in spreads can be precipitated by events that alter the relationship for individual securities[80] or whole sectors of the fixed income market. This chapter discusses sectors of the fixed income market that can provide opportunities for aggressive investors.

Investors mistakenly use the terms bonds[81] or bond market interchangeably when referring to corporate debt – a sector of the fixed income market that can provide opportunities for aggressive investors.

During normal market conditions, investment grade[82] corporate debt[83] trades at small yield spread to corresponding maturity Treasury security. When Mike Milken[84] reinvented the junk bond market in the early '80s, he unleashed a wave of leveraged buyouts (LBOs) that created a storm of "event risk"[85] causing credit

---

80 Some investors may recall event risk of the LBO era or the flight to quality panic of the 2008 financial crisis.

81 The term itself is misused; bonds are debt obligations of 10 yrs. or longer, most debt issued is 10 yrs. or less (notes).

82 Credit quality ratings Baa3 / BBB- or better.

83 Most of the corporate debt is 10 yrs. or less: notes not bonds.

84 Michael Milken, head of Drexel, Burnham Lambert high yield trading desk.

85 When the increased leverage of an LBO causes a rating down grade of the acquired company's outstanding debt.

downgrades that forced institutional investors to liquidate downgraded debt at prices attractive to aggressive investors.

Event risk opportunities disappeared after the 1991 collapse of the junk bond market and corporate debt spreads returned to normal until the late '08 financial crisis caused an extreme widening of spreads across the fixed income spectrum. During late '09, corporate debt spreads proceeded to narrow, reducing potential investment opportunities in the corporate debt market to credit upgrade candidates. When energy prices plunged in 2015, the specter of default risk returned to the corporate high yield market pushing spreads to levels the market hadn't seen since late '09.

Traditionally, the safest place to look for corporate debt opportunities is amongst credit upgrade candidates at or a notch below investment grade (Baa3/BBB-), securities in this credit rating range typically trade at yield spreads that provide investors compensation for higher levels of default risk: a credit rating upgrade will narrow the yield spread providing holders a potential capital gain in addition to the higher current yield.

Collateralized Mortgage Obligations (CMOs[86])

---

86 See Appendix 2 for an explanation of important CMO

are securities collateralized by conforming mortgage pools – structured to make monthly payments of interest and principal, they are the least understood sector of the fixed income market. To create CMOs, underwriters securitize pools of conforming mortgages via REMICs[87], into CMO tranches[88] engineered to exhibit predetermined patterns of principal paydown[89]. Interest rate gyrations impact CMOs' principal paydown speed and secondary market pricing, creating potential investment opportunities for aggressive investors.

CMO principal paydown is based on conforming mortgage 30-year amortization, numerous factors[90] can affect mortgage pool paydown, but interest rate changes are the most significant. Declining interest rates accelerate mortgage paydown and alter the maturity horizon for specific CMO tranches[91]: No one can accurately predict interest rate changes or mortgage pool paydown speeds so underwriters engineer all CMOs with an embedded call option that allows for partial or complete pay down within varying time horizons known as the call windows. When rising interest rates cause principal paydown to halt for support

---

characteristics.

87 Real Estate Mortgage Investment Conduit allows for the securitization of a mortgage pool.

88 Slice or piece of a mortgage pool.

89 Supports, TACs, PACs, etc.

90 Conforming mortgages are non-assumable and subject to early redemption from refinancing, sale, death, divorce, etc.

91 Support and TACs are companion tranches designed to keep PAC tranche call windows open.

tranche CMOs, the call window closes, and secondary market prices fall to account for the extended time horizon. Secondary market price declines of support tranche CMOs due to rising interest rates can create an investment opportunity. If interest rates return to previous levels the principal paydown horizon will shrink and the call window will reopen raising secondary market prices: CMOs exhibiting this type of interest rate driven price action are referred to as "story bonds" – the story being the potential interest rate drop that reopens the CMO call window and increases the secondary market price to par. The magnitude of an interest rate move can cause some "story bonds" to exhibit a double-digit rate of return[92]: This is an aggressive strategy dependent on the price movement of a security collateralized by agency backed mortgage pools, it is not without risk, the underlying mortgage collateral has agency backing but there is no guarantee of rapid principal prepayment. Investors should consult a financial adviser with CMO experience before attempting this investment strategy.

Municipal securities[93] offer investment opportunities for all defensive investors. Professionally managed Mutual funds, ETFs, and Closed End Funds (CEFs) owned by individuals are currently the largest holders of municipal

92 Interest plus principal payments.

93 See Chapter 7 of *Fixed Income Insights of a Bond Man* for a more complete discussion of municipal securities.

debt. Most investors are unaware funds often hold low rated securities[94] and utilize leverage[95] to boost current yield: a strategy that increases shareholder risk and reduces suitability for some investors. Defensive investors should consider individual issues.

Three types of municipal securities currently exist: General Obligation (G.O.s), Revenue, and Conduit[96] bonds. Strained state finances have shifted investors' preference from State G.O.s to essential service revenue bonds (water & sewer, hospitals, electric & gas). Frequently, essential service revenue issues under $10 million are overlooked by institutional investors, creating investment opportunities for defensive investors.

Since late 2009, small municipal issuers have had the opportunity to enroll in a mutual insurance organization for municipal issuers – Build America Mutual Assurance (BAM). Joining BAM, provides municipalities the ability to issue bonds with BAM's "AA" credit rating, reducing capital costs and providing defensive investors' a broader selection of small "AA" rated issuers.

---

94 Illinois, Kentucky, Michigan, New Jersey, Pennsylvania, Puerto Rico, etc.

95 Borrowed capital.

96 Appendix 4 provides important insights on conduit bonds.

Aggressive investors should investigate preferred stocks[97], a segment of the fixed income market that was popular during the 1990's only to be shunned after the 2008 financial market crisis and subsequent new banking regulations[98].

During the '90s, exchange traded[99] preferred stocks were issued by financial institutions to improve their balance sheet to comply with financial industry regulatory requirements, after the '08 financial crisis, regulations regarding what could be counted as financial institution Tier-1 or Tier-2 capital were modified that changed the investment attraction of this sector of the market.

Rising interest rates will eventually halt the long-running bull market for fixed income securities: Fixed-to-float and floating-rate preferred stocks can provide investors a hedge against rising interest rates.

Initially issued in the 1990's, fixed-to-float institutional preferred are perpetual securities that provide a fixed coupon for a specific number of years (5, 10, 15 etc.), after which an issuer can redeem the issue or reset the coupon to a predetermined rate[100], potentially limiting

---

97 See Chapter 8 of *Fixed Income Insights of a Bond Man* for a complete discussion of preferred stocks.

98 Dodd, Frank or Banking legislation.

99 Typically issued as callable perpetual preferred, their duration can be guesstimated.

100 The rate and reset mechanism are outlined in the offering document (prospectus).

interest rate risk.

The other variation of institutional preferred is a floating-rate security that is reset to a yield spread over a short-term benchmark, LIBOR[101] or a specific Treasury maturity: this type of preferred exhibits very little interest rate risk.

Currently, fixed-to-float and floating-rate securities dominate the institutional preferred market – the complexity of their structure makes it essential investors consult a financial adviser with experience in this sector of the fixed income market before investing.

---

101 London Inter-bank Offered Rate

Chapter 8:

Tradeable Derivatives

Financial derivatives: securities dependent upon the value of other securities, often invoke investor fear, yet investors fearlessly invest in derivative products such as mutual funds or ETFs. Chapter 4 advocated passive defensive investors utilize SPDRs[102] for equity exposure, this chapter discusses other derivative opportunities for aggressive investors.

SPDRs[103], holding more than $3 trillion of investors capital, is the largest, most widely held ETF of over 1500 U.S. based ETFs. Unfortunately, SPDRs' attractive features; trading liquidity, broad diversification, and low management fees[104] aren't features of most ETFs; many of which exhibit limited liquidity, high expense ratios, and employ leverage[105].

ETFs, like mutual funds, expand and contract their capital base[106] – during rising markets increased investor demand for ETFs shares expand its' capital base, forcing fund

---

102 A registered trademark of Standard & Poors Financial Services LLC.

103 ARCA symbol SPY

104 SPDRs gross expense ratio is 0.1102% and net expense ratio is 0.0945%.

105 To increase the capitalization or improve returns.

106 Like an accordion.

management to buy more of the underlying securities at rising prices – investor liquidation during market declines contracts an ETFs' capital base, forcing fund management to liquidate underlying securities as prices decline: ETFs' capital expansion and contraction magnify share price volatility. Additionally, many small ETFs also exhibit significant tracking errors (share prices that vary widely from NAV[107]) that aren't visible to investors. Alternatives to ETFs that provide opportunities to benefit from pricing errors exist for aggressive investors.

Closed end funds (CEFs) mentioned in Chapter 4 were introduced into the U.S. during the late 19th Century – throughout the early 20th Century they were more popular than mutual funds. Today's approximately 650 U.S. based CEFs' holding about $300 billion in assets[108] are an overlooked sector of the equity market.

Exchange traded CEFs' possess a capitalization structure similar to individual equities – after the public offering is completed the fund is exchange listed and the number of outstanding shares remains fixed[109], fund management seldom promotes the fund, leaving investors in the dark

---

107 NAV (net asset value) is calculated by dividing the fund's capitalization by the number of outstanding shares.

108 The capitalization of Apple Inc. at over $900 billion is three times that amount.

109 Some closed end funds have had rights offerings to raise more capital.

as to the fund's performance. Closed end funds fixed shares structure prevents ETFs' accordion like capitalization expansion and contraction induced price volatility, but CEFs' exhibit pricing anomalies that create investment opportunities.

CEFs are created with a wide range of investment strategies; from conservative (municipal funds) to aggressive; loan participation, high yield, single country, etc... Most investors are aware, equity market sectors can experience periods of popularity or disfavor that causes securities in a sector to exhibit extreme changes in valuation: market sector price volatility is reflected in closed end fund share prices.

Unlike ETFs' hidden price tracking errors, CEFs' market price trade at a discount or premium to NAV that is continuously disclosed to investors. Typically, CEFs are priced at discounts ranging from zero to 10%, and often exhibit their largest NAV discount during the last weeks of the year. CEFs provide investors the opportunity to benefit from discount compression, price appreciation[110] and attractive dividend yield: always establish a realistic goal and time horizon before investing.

---

110 Price rebound after year-end tax-loss selling subsides as the New Year market rallies.

Exchange traded equity options[111], commonly referred to as puts & calls, were the innovative financial product of the early 1970's. Prior to exchange listing, equity options traded in a cumbersome manner via custom contracts between counter parties. In 1973, the Chicago Board Option Exchange (CBOE) Clearing Corporation[112] standardized equity option contracts; the number of shares, strike prices, expiration dates, exercise process, margin requirements, etc., and became the central counterparty for all CBOE[113] exchange trade options. The CBOE's trading platform for OCC's option contracts provided rapid price dissemination, improved market liquidity, and pricing efficiency – backed by the CBOE's aggressive investor relations campaign option trading volume rapidly expanded.

The short-term nature[114] of equity options make them a natural fit for speculative traders, but option contracts require someone willing to take the opposite side of the trade: The OCC only acts as the counterparty between the option seller and buyer, it does not take the opposite side of the trade.

---

111 A six-year association with a broker dealer specializing in option trading provided valuable insights.

112 Changed to the Options Clearing Corp. (OCC) in 1975.

113 Chicago Board Option Exchange

114 Equity options were originally offered in 3,6- & 9-month cycles, Long-Term Equity Anticipation Securities (LEAPS) weren't introduced until 1990.

Investors write / sell a covered call against an equity holding, creating a new option contract, generating income (for the seller), and increases option contract open interest: the call option buyer is speculating or hedging a short position.

Option premiums are a product of a number of factors; the main ones are how far the strike price is in or out of the money[115], the amount of time (days) to expiration, interest rates (the cost of money), and the expected volatility of the underlying equity. Volatile market conditions can rapidly change the risk / reward trade-off for option premiums[116] – all of which makes option trading a speculative enterprise.

Covered call writing is a conservative strategy to generate income and provide downside protection for an equity position: the maximum return on a covered call write occurs when the underlying security is called away, but declining interest rates have reduced premiums, shrinking potential returns on covered call writes[117], and reduced its' attraction.

The early 1980's development of index options[118],

---

115 The amount the equity priced above or below the strike price, this is an inverse relationship for puts & calls.

116 Option premiums often exhibit high volatility.

117 Simultaneous buying of an equity followed by writing calls against the new position.

118 Index options are cash settlement.

provided investors a convenient way to hedge portfolios against adverse market moves. Portfolio hedging has an associated cost that can limit portfolio returns, but it can also provide investment flexibility. Investors with low cost basis / high dividend yield portfolios[119] can protect their capital gains while maintaining their portfolio's income stream by buying in the money index puts as an insurance policy: In the event of a market sell-off the index puts will move dollar for dollar with the index generating a gain that offsets the portfolio price decline while the investor continues to receive the dividend income.

During an equity market rise, purchasing in the money index call options requires less capital than purchasing an equal share amount of the SPDRs ETF, allowing investors to quickly increase equity exposure: In the money call options move dollar for dollar with the index, generating a gain that will offset the higher price to acquire SPDRs or individual equities.

Investors anticipating an equity market decline can sell in the money index puts[120] using Treasury securities to cover margin requirements: a strategy that generates option premium and interest income. Put options expiring prior to a market decline can be written

---

119 Recall the recommendation for long term investors to buy high cash flow equities with rapidly growing dividends.

120 The put strike price is above the index level.

further out in time, generating another premium.

Index options are speculative: read the OCC prospectus carefully and consider all risks before committing capital.

Chapter 9:

Closing Thoughts

The end of company sponsored defined benefit pension plans during the 1980's, forcing inexperienced investors to assume responsibility for their retirement funds, uncovered an investment knowledge void the financial services industry was happy to exploit with a myriad of products designed to generate perpetual profits for product sponsors at the expense of investors' returns. This book is intended to provide investors the information needed to make intelligent investment decisions.

Successful retirement investing requires a strategy that combines risk control while minimizing costs. Investors lacking risk control often panic during market meltdowns, foolishly moving capital amongst high cost investment alternatives in the hope of reducing portfolio risk. Defensive investing strategy is designed to control portfolio risk while reducing associated costs – it is a rational alternative to the managed products and accounts touted by many financial advisers. Investors with minimal investment experience or time can easily implement a passive defensive strategy via an index ETF (SPDRs) and Treasury securities as outlined in this book. Passive defensive investor's only time requirements are determining risk tolerance to initially established portfolio asset allocation and re-balancing portfolio allocations when they deviate by more than 10% from predetermined levels. Aggressive defensive investors that have carefully quantified their risk tolerance and appropriate portfolio asset allocations can creatively utilize their time and knowledge to actively participate in the financial markets.

Forty-years of financial services industry experience provided anecdotal insights to Chapter 1's rules:

Take your ego out of the decision process: the 3rd Rule.

Everyone makes mistakes, stubbornness makes a bad situation worse. Many investors develop what psychologist refer to as "sunk cost syndrome", causing them to see a losing position out to the bitter end regardless of the outcome. "It's OK to be wrong, it's not OK to stay wrong" – "Your first loss is your least loss": create liquidity and move on to the next opportunity[121].

Companies go through a life cycle – securities you inherited from relatives may not be appropriate holdings: Control your emotions and analyze an inheritance as carefully as you would

---

121 The 1st rule don't lose money refers to a large percentage of the portfolio, so keep the loss small to uphold the 1st rule.

a potential new investment.

Fear and greed are emotions investors must control. Greed impairs risk control during an equity market rise as downside risk is rapidly increasing: Liquidating positions into a market rise accumulates capital that can be reinvested after a market sell-off. Fear takes control during market panics making it difficult to commit capital when prices are attractive: Market panics provide opportunities for investors that controlled their risk during the market rise.

Never allow an investment decision to be contingent on other decisions, analyze each decision on its' merits.

Be flexible; the 4th rule.

Not selling a security to avoid paying taxes is as foolish as riding a losing position into the ground. Investors often proclaim they can't sell because they can't afford to pay the taxes: Wait long enough and the next market sell-off will solve the tax problem.

A long-time horizon can generate large capital gains – unfortunately, most individual investors have a limited time horizon and can face unexpected liquidity needs, rising prices provide an opportunity to create liquidity. Capital gains aren't real until they are realized – verify the downside risk of holding a position before passing up an opportunity to realize profits.

Investors frequently “stick to what they know” overlooking securities or sectors of the markets that have fallen out of favor. Investors should strive to increase their investment knowledge by devoting time to research unfamiliar sectors of the market.

Appendix 1:

Yield Calculations

Interest rates and bond prices are inversely related. When interest rates decline, bond prices rise – conversely, as interest rates rise, bond prices decline. Interest rate change affects current yield and yield to maturity.

The current yield calculation is as follows:

Current Yield = Dollar Amount of Annual Coupon / Current Price, or

Face Value = Dollar Amount of Coupon /Coupon Rate

Dollar Amount of Coupon = Coupon Rate times Face Value

Current yield calculations don't account for the reinvestment value of future cash flows, i.e. interest and principal, for that a yield to maturity calculation is required. Calculated by hand, yield to maturity is a cumbersome reiteration calculation:

Approximate Yield to Maturity = C+ (FV-CP/n)

/ (FV+CP)/2

C = Coupon express as actual annual dollar amount

FV = Face Value, typically par or $1,000.00

PV= Present Value

N = number of years to maturity

The approximate yield to maturity rate is utilized as (*i*) in the present value calculation to see how close it comes to the market price.

PV = FV / (1 + *i*)n

PV = Present Value i.e. market price

FV = Face Value, typically par or $1,000.00

i = interest rate you are looking for to make the PV calculation = market price

n = number of years to maturity and the number of times (1 +*i*) is multiplied by itself.

If the calculation doesn't equal the bond's current market price, recalculate using a new value for the variable (i) until the calculation equals the market price, i.e. the yield to maturity.

Prior to electronic calculators, reiteration calculations were done by hand for increments of one-eighth of a percent to over ten percent across forty-years and published in a book appropriately titled *The Yield Book*. The advent of modern calculators allowed professionals and individuals to quickly calculate yield to maturity for any set of variables. Today, the internet provides websites that allow for accurate yield to maturity calculation.

Investors should understand the yield to maturity calculation and how coupon reinvestment rate impacts total return.

Appendix 2:

Understanding Agency CMOs

Chapter 4 briefly discussed Agency securities; specifically, Agency backed CMOs, a misunderstood sector of the Fixed Income markets. The following discussion provides information investors need before deciding if CMOs are a suitable investment.

Safety of Principal

Ginnie Mae is part of HUD[122], the mortgage collateral backing Ginnie Mae CMOs are backed by the full faith and credit of the U.S. Treasury. Fannie Mae & Freddie Mac are currently operated in conservatorship by the FHFA (Federal Housing Finance Agency). Under FHFA conservatorship, Fannie & Freddie mortgage collateral has an implied backing of the U.S. Treasury. With the U.S. Treasury standing behind the timely payment of interest and principal of underlying mortgages, CMO holders will ultimately see a return of principal along with interest. All CMOs have an embedded call option. Buyers of CMOs at par (100) or less cannot lose money if the security is held to maturity, buyers of CMOs at a premium (par+) could experience an early call which reduces the effective yield of the security.

---

122 Housing and Urban Development is an Agency of the Federal Government.

Yield

Agency CMOs typically trade at a positive yield spread to the corresponding maturity Treasury security – CMOs' higher yield is compensation for the uncertainty of final maturity. Mortgage collateral paydown rates can substantially change, impacting the time horizon and the effective yield for CMO holders. Time horizon risk is the main reason for the higher yield CMOs exhibit.

Liquidity

Agency CMOs are self-liquidating securities that pay holders monthly cash flow consisting of interest and principal over the life of the security. Changing mortgage pool principal paydown rates can temporarily halt principal paydown, effectively extending the life of CMOs backed by the pool. While CMOs are trade-able, pricing depends on several factors such as interest rates, mortgage collateral, and paydown speed.

Maturity

CMOs are structured to pay monthly interest and principal: monthly interest payments will be reduced as the mortgage pool principal is reduced. Investors wishing to maintain interest income need to reinvest the returned principal. During rapidly rising interest rates, CMOs can exhibit extension risk that causes a sharp reduction in principal payments: mortgage collateral coupon rate is an important factor.

Appendix 3:

Credit Ratings

Moody's, Standard & Poors, Fitch, and DBRS are referred to as the big four credit ratings services. All four are certified as a Nationally Recognized Statistical Rating Organization (NRSR0)[123] by the Securities Exchange Commission (SEC). Moody's and Standard & Poors ratings are the two names most investors recognize for fixed income ratings. Listed below are the long-term rating scales for the 4 largest rating services:

Moody's DBRS[124]	S&P	Fitch	
Aaa	AAA	AAA	AAA
Aa1 (high)	AA+	AA+	AA
Aa2	AA	AA	AA
Aa3 (low)	AA−	AA−	AA
A1 (high)	A+	A+	A

123 The other firms are A. M. Best Company Inc., Egan-Jones Rating Co., Japan Credit Rating Agency Ltd., Kroll Bond Rating Agency, HR Ratings de Mexico S.A. and Morningstar Credit Ratings LLC.
124 DBRS, founded in 1976 and originally known as Dominion Bond Rating Service is certified a NRSRO.

A2	A	A	A
A3 (low)	A–	A–	A
Baa1 (high)	BBB+	BBB+	BBB
Baa2	BBB	BBB	BBB
Baa3 (low)	BBB–	BBB–	BBB
Ba1 (high)	BB+	BB+	BB
Ba2	BB	BB	BB
Ba3 (low)	BB–	BB–	BB
B1 (high)	B+	B+	B
B2	B	B	B
B3 (low)	B–	B–	B
Caa1 (high)	CCC+		CCC
Caa2	CCC	CCC	CCC
Caa3 (low)	CCC-		CCC
(high)			CC
Ca	CC		CC
(low)			CC
C	C		
		DDD	

		DD	
	D	D	D
NR	NR	NR (Not Rated)	
	R (Regulatory supervision)		
	SD	RD (Selective Default)	
WR (Withdrawn)			
U	U (Unsolicited Rating)		

Above the dotted line at Baa3/BBB– is investment grade; below the line is sub-investment grade (High Yield aka Junk Bonds).

Credit ratings are not carved in stone: an issue's ratings can vary over the life of the issue due to changes in the issuer's financial status or technology that changes the dynamics of an industry.

Credit rating agencies typically perform quarterly reviews of corporate finances, occasionally placing individual issuers on positive or negative "credit watch". An issuer's credit rating can change at any time – portfolio management is a dynamic process.

Appendix 4:

Redefining Municipal Bonds

Conduit financing is a politically controversial form of municipal finance. Conduit bonds are revenue bonds issued to fund a private entity deemed to have a "public purpose"; such as hospitals, nursing homes, and low income public housing developments: projects that are financially questionable as evidenced by the higher occurrence of default highlighted in a Moody's study.[125]

Conduit bond issuance is intended to reduce financing costs of not for profit enterprises that provide necessary services, it is also employed to finance the construction of sports stadiums & exhibition halls: When the financed facilities are privately owned, the bond issue is classified as Alternative Minimum Tax[126] (AMT) and the interest is not tax-exempt for all holders.

The political logic behind conduit bond issuance is local job creation, it is also an alternative to offering tax breaks or other incentives to sports franchise owners contemplating relocating their

---

125 http://www.municipalbonds.com/education/read/77/default-rates-of-municipal-bonds

126 AMT: Alternative Minimum Tax is a minimum tax imposed on individuals, corporations, trusts, and estates with adjusted income above a threshold amount.

franchise. Investors need to understand conduit bonds are usually not an obligation of a municipality.

Some municipalities opt to build and maintain sports facilities leased to sports franchises. If leasing fees fail to cover the municipality's operating costs, the municipality adds these expenses to its yearly operating budget, potentially making municipal owned stadiums a burden to the local taxpayers.

Multi-family low income housing is another questionable use of conduit financing. Section 8, of the Housing Act of 1937, provides government funded housing vouchers for low income individuals. The Federal Government's definition of low income has been employed by real-estate developers to qualify projects for conduit financing by setting aside a percentage of apartments for a period of twenty-years to residents with incomes sufficiently below an area's median income. After twenty-years, the Section 8 restrictions expire, and the property can be refinanced or sold. Real-estate developers wouldn't undertake a project they didn't expect to be profitable, yet the previously cited Moody's study indicated housing bond issues have a higher default rate: making them inappropriate for investors that prioritize preservation of capital over current income.

The higher coupon yield of conduit bonds can

divert investors' attention from comparably rated municipal G.O., or revenue bonds. Conduit bond holders own a security with quasi tax-exempt income[127] that lacks the backing of a municipal taxing authority to cover timely payment of interest and principal. Conduit bonds can be likened to high yield debt (junk bonds): holders of these securities accept business risk for a fixed coupon interest payment. Municipal investors typically don't structure their portfolio to accommodate for defaults that accompany this type of high yield investing.[128]

127 Often only partial tax-exemption due to AMT.
128 Recall the discussion of the underlying principle of high yield investing as laid out in Professor Frederick Macaulay's 1938 book *The Movement of Interest Rates, Bond Yields and Stock Prices in the United States since 1856.*

Appendix 5:

Insights to Quantifying Equity Valuation

Investors often utilize two equity parameters: Price/Earnings ratio (P/E ratio [price per share divided by 12-month earnings per share]) and dividend yield (annual per share dividend divided by the price per share) – how each is utilized is dependent on an investor's priority of growth or income.

P/E ratios can have a range of values depending upon which 12-months are used for the calculation; trailing 12-months, current calendar year earnings assumption, forward 12-months, or previous 6-months + projected 6-months.

Defensive investing originally advocated using "normalized" earnings[129] to calculate a "margin of safety" P/E ratio: equities approach this valuation level during all-out market panics. More importantly, the "normalized" earnings calculation views corporate earnings as cyclical, it didn't anticipate future earnings growth. Investors typically buy equities based on potential earnings growth, which is utilized when calculating forward P/E expectations. Trailing 12-month earnings calculations don't estimate

---

129 A 10-year earnings average.

forward-looking guidance for an equity's P/E ratio, investors should calculate a P/E ratio based on a realistic forward-looking earnings estimate.

The rate of dividend increase provides an important insight to equity valuation many investors overlook. Income-oriented investors attempt to maximize current income by owning high current dividend yield equities – corporations in the mature stage of their life cycle and royalty trusts. Chapter 6 suggested equities exhibiting high levels of cash flow and rapidly rising dividends were better long-term investments. Cash dividends are typically paid from available capital[130], corporations paying rapidly growing dividends typically exhibit high free cash flow[131], a true indicator of earnings growth and future price appreciation.

Investment services provide statistics on dividend growth and screens of their data base that list companies exhibiting the fastest earnings and dividend growth rates. While dividend growth rate isn't the only indicator investors should consider, it is an overlooked predictor of earnings growth and price appreciation potential.

---

130 Assuming the corporation doesn't borrow to meet dividend payments.

131 Cash left after reinvestment in plant, equipment, marketing, new product research, etc.

Earnings yield, the inverse of the P/E ratio, can be compared to Treasury yields as a valuation indicator. Theoretically, a corporation can have an infinite life (equities are long duration securities), current convention is to compare the S&P 500 Equity Index earnings yield to the 10-year Treasury note yield. Treasury securities don't exhibit equities default risk: Under normal market scenarios, equities should exhibit higher earnings yields[132] than the 10-year Treasury note yield.

Investors can gain important insights by studying the relationship between earnings yield and P/E ratio. Equities trading at 10-times earnings have an earnings yield of 10%, while equities trading at 20-times earnings have an earnings yield of 5%: rising P/E ratios equate to falling earnings yield like the inverse relationship between interest rates and bond prices. Assuming other market factors remain the same, interest rate moves that affect bond pricing / current yield also affect the spread relationship between earnings yield and the 10-yr. Treasury note yield: During interest rate declines, for the spread between the equity market's earnings yield and the 10-year Treasury note yield to remain unchanged, equity prices need to increase. Conversely when Treasury yields rise, equity prices need to decline for spread to remain unchanged.

---

132 Trade at a positive yield spread to the corresponding maturity Treasury security.

Fixed income spread relationships change with market conditions: The spread relationship between equity yields and the 10-year Treasury note yield changes with equity market sentiment – rising equity prices often cause compression of the equity market P/E ratio and the 10-yr. Treasury note yield spread as the equity market becomes over-valued.

Equity yield and the corresponding spread to the 10-year Treasury note is an accurate indicator of valuation when calculated for a market index rather than an individual equity. Individual securities exhibit security specific risk and can deviate from market averages due to business specific or industry related reasons.

About the Author

Mark J. Angioletti has worked as a Registered Rep. in the Financial Services Industry for more than 40 years. Mr. Angioletti holds a Series 7 General Securities License, a Series 63 Uniform Securities License, a Series 53 Municipal Securities Principal License, and a Series 65 Registered Investment Adviser License.

The author can be contacted at mjangioletti@gmail.com

Made in the USA
Monee, IL
05 November 2026

67811482R00046